SuperMoon Frequency

Beizhonn Davis

BookLeaf Publishing

India | USA | UK

Presentation by *BookLeaf Publishing*

Web: www.bookleafpub.com

E-mail: info@bookleafpub.com

ISBN: 9789363301627

First edition 2024

This is in dedication to my aunt Tonia, You will always be loved and missed!

Room 222

The night is young, The air is still. I breathe you in so I can heal. Smoke fills my lungs, is this for real? No cameras here just lies and reels. The truth comes out, We start to fight, My wrongs are wrongs and your wrong is right. How can we stop this back and forth? Let's just move forward and pass the torch. In Room 222 I come alive, Realizing my worth is more than just a demise. Emotional turmoil, Intensity rise. Angel numbers appear everytime we lock eyes.

Supermoon Frequency

The frequency of my energy is flowing through a full moon. When it's closest to the earth I feel kissed by the universe. The wind blows violently on a quiet night and yet I feel the vibes from the supermoon. Making me to feel empowered and beautiful, My skin glows with the intensity of the moons shadow side. Seeing how the frequency is in alignment with my souls purpose, I can inhale the good karma that has taken lifetimes of me crossing paths. I say hello to my life path number eight, And shake hands with the past that has taught me so much in many different dimensions. As the supermoon frequency embodies an hourglass sitting beside me, I can finally flip and reset the sand that escapes from times existence. A new portal, Renewed mentality. Sitting above the water staring down as the influence rips through the tides, We are a supermoon.

Detox

When the mind is clear and all doubts are erased, one can sleep peacefully without a soul full of hate. As much as the darkness seeps in, Clouds begin to surround the aura, We sit with our own boxes filled with many different pandoras. Detox the mind and the soul will decompress, On the journey to enlightenment and success.

September Truths

As the leaves change and transition, The winds of september come upon us. Seeking truth in the middle of a season where life often becomes unresolved. Looking towards new beginnings and a fulfilling journey, The truths we allow to flow will be the opening to a dark and cold healing. When the ground is solid and the moon is full, I pray you break free from the silence that keeps you warm in september. With my hoodie pulled up and crisp air leaving my breath, I hope you find the heart to release your expectations.

Flag Day

Show me the flag that displays my emotions, I need the key to unlock this forbidden fabric that shows my inner duality. Let it fly high and be proud on days like this, Where motivation to be yourself can be misplaced. This flag is stitched so intricately to represent the desires within your highest self. Let it be the veins that circulate throughout your system, Flowing to your heart and letting you know that your presence here is justified.

Underestimate

You underestimated the depths of my soul. As I awake to another choice, Another chance to express my thoughts without hesitation. As we celebrate a new dawn, You overlooked the affection of my words and actions. We get use to those weights that hold us underneath the ocean, To think I've drowned and couldn't pull myself out of those cold waters is a disservice.

Crown

Somehow this crown can bear all of the gravity against it. There's something vaguely memorable about the presence of such a bold headdress. When the universe chooses you it's safe to embrace it as a compliment. Give thanks to the constellations, As the stars dance above our heads in unison. Grab ahold of the gems that adorn your head, Send your kiss to the moon and it shall come right back ten fold. Let your crown lead you to your next destination with beautiful discernment.

Candle to flame

This candle ignites the pathway to a new lesson of this lifetime. As the rain gently pours down the windshield of my eyes, I see the flame dancing above the wick in my room. No shadows are there to disturb nature's alchemy, Only peacefulness fills the air as the flame continues to move about. Praying that this will never burn out and remain shining it's light until eternity exists within the shadow realm. Such a void could not exist without the darkness to attach with it. The wax will continue to replenish itself as it melts down showing how we could have a temporary forever.

Clarity walk

On the tracks racing to receiving a moment of clarity. When the mind is clouded like a storm waiting to invade an open field. Walking through nature's playground, Releasing every once of doubt, confusion and sometimes the good times. Meditation within it's purest form of peacefulness, Everyday the moments of life should be filled with free will such as this.

Meditate

It becomes loud in here as I ignite the heavens greenest herbs. There's no meditation more complete as we inhale together. We exchange thoughts from one look, We both innerstand the flow of energy that comes with this chemistry. This chemistry overcomes every ounce of our success in different realms. Focused on every breath and becoming one with the divine source is a feeling of deeply seated trust. Meditation is the medicine of a person in need of a sound mind.

Zen Palace

I want to go to zen palace where everything is irreplaceable. Show me the many moods of a person who has never seen what it's like to remain in nirvana. The planets are consistently evolving, As do I when the stillness shows how quiet the mind can get. Once the mind becomes closed away from the outside world, You find diamonds in a meditative state that keeps your heart inside of the richness and outside of the negativity.

New Moon

One new goal a day is a beautiful landmark. To complete and set intentions for a new beginning. A new project to dive and pull yourself by the reigns of our planetary alignment. I look to the moon everyday as validation from the galaxy's to proceed with letting the moon hijack our emotions. The new moon weighs on me heavily like a ton of bricks weighing down my soul. The new moon doesn't owe us anything, Living with a new ability of intuition and divine guidance. Nothing can get in the way of a lunar attachment, The intimacy grows with each phase and like a soul tie each phase has given us deep affection.

Flower Bed

Lay down in your flower bed of temporary emotions. Roses grow thorn like stems to imitate the aggression of the past. Let the sunlight penetrate through the darkness of the soil and hope that the flowers of your smile continues to grow. As the leaves fall off into the bed, Let the flower expose all of its beauty in it's entirety.

Sand

As the sand reaches the bottom of the hour glass,
Time is no longer a virtue. Staring into the abyss
of a new chapter, I let the sand slip through my
fingers. Justifying that my time here is to late.
When a new hour glass is in the present moment
it signifies not to let those moments slip away.
Just like sand from the earth, I leave my prints
on every grain and every grain is a sign of life
existing in photographic memory.

Admiration

Waterfalls are so close to an emotional element. I marvel at the beauty of it all, there's nothing quite like the mountain peaks and valleys of this earth that remain so profound. Gazing in awe at the beautiful plains of this earth, I bow my head in honor of God's creation. There is nothing greater than experiencing every corner of this space with such a gentle soul. As we hold hands with every mountain, and share whispers of the willows around us. I can't help but to stand in admiration of all the things known and unknown.

Disconnected

Sitting in silence like the monks do, Feeling unplugged and readily unavailable. In the dark is where solitude can be found amongst men who dwell in clouded judgement. The dark clouds hang over heads like a teleprompter, Looking to read the next sentence with no sign of light. Social platforms diminish with every crippling pain of anxiety and sometimes happiness can be found based on the circumstance. Detach the mind and separate the heart from truth, Seek and you will find you! Isolate the hurt and abandon the tears, A wave of letting go is coming near. Beneath the shadow self is unresolved traumas, Lean into the healing waters and unlink from the unwavering vibes that linger over in your sleep like a paralysis monster. Open up the gates to an awakening, Channel your chakra of colors to paint a program of separation.

Chakras

Energy fields surround me like oxygen with
nowhere to go. Outlets of different auras seeking
to find a colorful palette to inch its paintbrush.
One of them are out of balance seeking to find
comfort like a mother to it's child. The chakras
that exist within lead to a harmonious tornado,
Circling inside like a moth to a flame.

Spirituality

Invoking the highest and benevolent vigor.
Opening a path for uninterrupted peace, Giving
thanks to the divine essence of a higher
understanding. The laws in place were made to
he honored in such a way that even animals
recognize the balances. Walking off the edge of
uncertainty, Knowing in your heart that what's
true doesn't always need to be proved but can be
felt with every intention. This blessing that
approaches us at the time of birth, Each one
special. Signing a soul contract before exiting
the womb of the divine feminine. The deja Vu of
life always seems to make hair follicles stand up
as if you were being haunted. Spirituality awaits
like a guide expecting to be the medium that
leads us over and out of purgatory